THE Holy Ghost

DISCOVERING YOUR EXTRAORDINARY NEW GIFT

CATHERINE CHRISTENSEN & JANE DELVE

CFI
AN IMPRINT OF CEDAR FORT, INC.
SPRINGVILLE, UTAH

ISBN 13: 978-1-4621-1868-7

Published by CFI, an imprint of Cedar Fort, Inc.
2373 W. 700 S., Springville, UT 84663
Distributed by Cedar Fort, Inc., www.cedarfort.com

LIBRARY OF CONGRESS CONTROL NUMBER: 2016945329

Cover and interior design by Shawnda T. Craig

Edited by Rebecca Bird

Printed in the United States of America

10 9 8 7 6 5 4 3 2 1

Printed on acid-free paper

TAP IN YOUR AGE.

To be baptized and receive the gift of the Holy Ghost, you need to be (at least) 8 years old.

If you tapped in 8 or older into the age calculator, then brilliant! This book is especially for you! If you tapped in younger, then don't worry—this book is still great for you, as you are preparing for baptism. Whatever your age, after completing this book, you'll be super prepared to feel and use the power of the Holy Ghost in your life!

You have been given the BEST GIFT EVER from Heavenly Father: the Holy Ghost!

If you know how to use it, this incredible gift will change your life forever in wonderful, amazing ways. It means that you are never alone. But how do you use this special gift? The Holy Ghost does not have a simple "ON" button. It can take time and practice to hear and recognize the Holy Ghost talking to you. But this book can help you figure it out! Read on for fun activities, quizzes, tips, pictures, and general awesome stuff to help you use the Holy Ghost in your life!

ALL ABOUT ME...

Name: ______________________

Age: ______________________

Baptismal Date: ______________

Confirmed By: _______________

Best Friend: ________________

Best Talent: ________________

Favorite Treat: ______________

Favorite Color: ______________

USING THE HOLY GHOST

Have you ever felt:

- ☐ Scared
- ☐ Frightened
- ☐ Anxious
- ☐ Lonely
- ☐ Angry
- ☐ Inadequate

If you have, the Holy Ghost can help you deal with these difficult feelings in your life—and this book will show you how!

— ICONS —

You will see these icons throughout the book. Here's what they mean.

Expert Tips: Brilliant advice from prophets and leaders about how to use the Holy Ghost. These people know what they are talking about!

Crafts, games, and other exciting activities that you can try with family or friends. Perfect for FHE or just for fun!

Fill in the blanks, answer questions, and write about your experiences with the Holy Ghost.

Read stories and advice about the Holy Ghost from children like you.

MORE ABOUT ME...

Where I want to serve my mission:

____

What I want to do when I'm older:

____

My favorite scripture story & why:

____

____

The Holy Ghost appeared as a dove when Jesus Christ got baptized. A dove symbolizes peace. Flip the pages of the book, and watch the dove fly.

Can you draw a sun?

Can you finish this picture by adding more doves?

Receiving the Holy Ghost

ARE YOU READY TO BE BAPTIZED & CONFIRMED?

WHAT AN EXCITING STEP!

Complete the checklist so you can be prepared for such an important day.

- ☐ Meet with your bishop.
- ☐ Read three scriptures about the Holy Ghost.
- ☐ Read three conference talks about the Holy Ghost.
- ☐ Set a baptismal and confirmation date.
- ☐ Talk with parents or someone close to you about your feelings about getting baptized and confirmed.
- ☐ Get white baptismal clothes.
- ☐ Turn 8 years old.
- ☐ Read about your baptismal covenant in your *Faith in God* book.
- ☐ Fast and pray on your baptism and confirmation day to help you be more spiritually ready.

"I am excited to get baptized because everyone in my family has been baptized except me. I think it will make me feel warm and nice. The Holy Ghost will tell me the right things to do, and when I get scared, I know He will help my fears to go away."

Matthew, age 7, Wales, UK

Baptism puts you on the right path back to Heavenly Father. In this maze, find the correct path to get to the end!

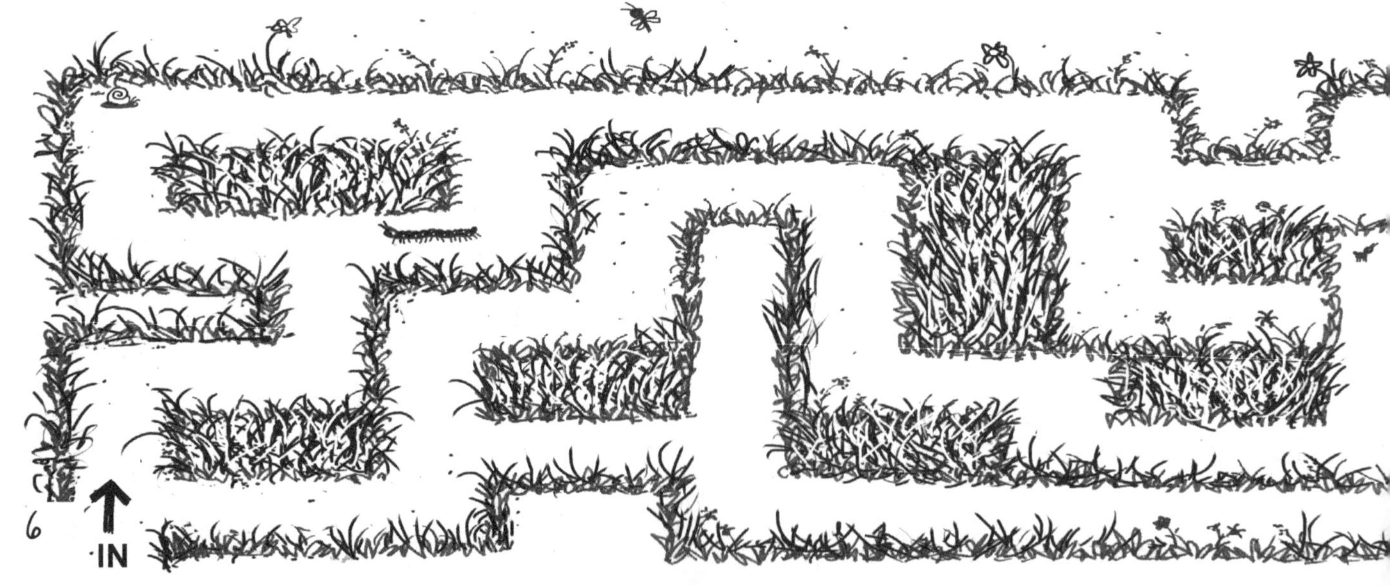

Before you are baptized, you can feel the power of the Holy Ghost, but you don't have the full gift. After you are baptized and confirmed, you get upgraded to the full, wonderful gift of the Holy Ghost. Here are a few of the differences:

POWER OF THE HOLY GHOST	GIFT OF THE HOLY GHOST
Can be felt before baptism	Is given during confirmation
Is felt on occasion	Can be a constant companion
Comes only to witness of truth	Witnesses, comforts, guides, warns, protects, teaches, sanctifies, reminds
Can be felt by anyone	Can only be felt by those confirmed

Expert Tip: "The Holy Ghost is such an uplifting power and source of necessary gospel knowledge that to have his constant companionship and influence is the greatest gift a person can receive in mortality." Joseph Fielding McConkie, http://eom.byu.edu/index.php/Holy_Ghost.

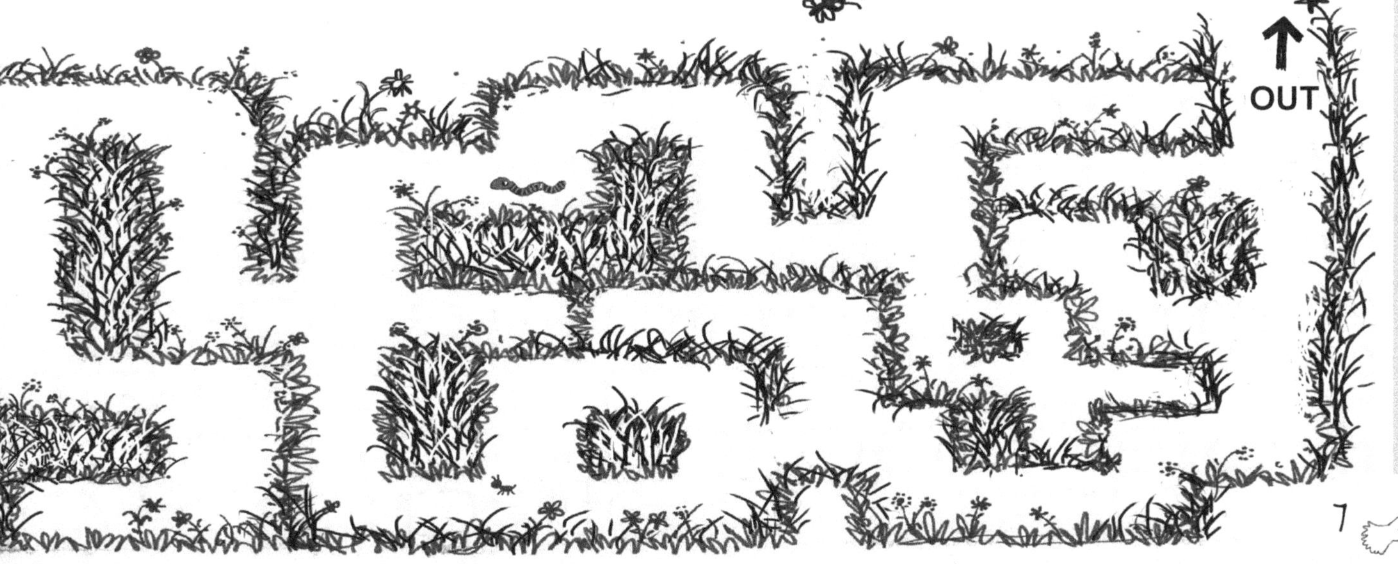

RECEIVING THE HOLY GHOST

The following are steps to receiving your gift, but they are out of order! Number each picture inside the gray box in the correct order of how you receive the Holy Ghost.

A

Learn how to recognize, listen to, and use your new gift.

B

Get confirmed as a member of the Church and receive the gift of the Holy Ghost.

C

Dry off (optional, but recommended).

D

Sit down while Melchizedek Priesthood holders lay hands on your head.

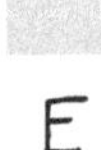

Get baptized into the Church of Jesus Christ of Latter-day Saints.

E

Answer Key: A-5, B-4, C-2, D-3, E-1

YOUR CONFIRMATION

How did you feel when priesthood leaders placed their hands on your head?

____

____

Who gave you the blessing and confirmation?

____

What do you remember about what was said in your blessing?

____

____

____

Check how you felt:

- [ ] Happy
- [ ] Tingly
- [ ] Warm
- [ ] Spiritual
- [ ] Full of light
- [ ] Brought to tears
- [ ] Other: ______________________

DRAW A PICTURE OF YOU GETTING CONFIRMED

"Today I got baptized. It was very special for me. The most special part for me was getting the gift of the Holy Ghost. Daddy put his hands on my head and said, "I say unto you, receive the Holy Ghost." Right after he said that, I felt this warm feeling start from my head, all the way down to my toes. Then I knew that the Holy Ghost is something real, and I knew the Church is true. I felt so happy. I felt the Spirit with me the rest of the night."

Jalena, age 8, Washington, USA

BAPTISMAL COVENANTS

By getting baptized, you make A COVENANT WITH HEAVENLY FATHER. He knows that you are now ready to make those important promises and do your very best to keep them. That's a lot of responsibility! But, as always, Heavenly Father wants to help you. He sends you the Holy Ghost to guide you to keep your promises and to prompt you to repent if you break any of the promises. So what are the promises you make at baptism?

A covenant is a special promise that you make with Heavenly Father. It is a two-way promise. You promise to obey Heavenly Father and He promises great blessings in return.

Your BAPTISMAL PROMISES are found in the SACRAMENT PRAYER.

Fill in the blanks on the sacrament prayer to read about your baptismal covenants. (Hint: If you need help, look up D&C 20:77.)

O God, the ________ Father, we _____ thee in the name of thy _____, Jesus ________, to bless and _________ this bread to the ______ of all those who partake of it, that they may eat in ________________ of the body of thy _____, and witness unto thee, O God, the Eternal ________, that

[Promise 1] they are ________ to take upon them the _______ of thy Son, and

[Promise 2] always ___________ him and

[Promise 3] keep his __________________ which he has given them; that

[Promise 4] they may always have his ________ to be with them. Amen.

See promises 1, 2, and 3 in the sacrament prayer you filled out, then match them to some examples of what those promises mean.

YOU PROMISE

Promise 1: ______________________________

____

Promise 2: ______________________________

____

Promise 3: ______________________________

____

THIS MEANS:

Keeping Jesus in your thoughts throughout the day. *For example, saying little prayers in your head, wearing a CTR ring.*

Choosing the right. *For example, keeping the Sabbath day holy, obeying parents, not lying or stealing.*

Trying to be like Jesus by doing what He would do. *For example, serving others, treating everyone kindly, sharing the gospel.*

HEAVENLY FATHER PROMISES

Promise 4: That you will ALWAYS have His Spirit to be with you!

That's what this book is all about!

FOCUSING ON THE SACRAMENT

- Make a goal of one thing you can do better this week.
- Read your scriptures or illustrated scripture stories.
- Read the *Friend* magazine.
- Draw scripture stories, especially ones about Jesus.
- Say a prayer. In particular, ask forgiveness for your mistakes from the week.
- Quietly read the words to songs in the *Children's Songbook* or the hymnbook.

NOW YOU KNOW what your baptismal covenants are; the tricky part is figuring out how to keep those covenants every day. In the following situations, how should you react to keep your promises and have the Holy Ghost with you?

1. To your surprise, your friend starts swearing. ________________________________
2. A person you know shows you something on her phone that makes you feel very uncomfortable. ________________________________
3. Everyone is teasing a girl at school. She appears to be friendless and alone. You know that if you talk to her, others may tease you too. ________________________________
4. You are listening to some music through some headphones, then you realize the song contains swearing. No one can hear what you are listening to. ________________________________
5. You are in a shop and are given too much change, but you don't notice until you are halfway home. ________________________________
6. You are watching your favorite show and your mom insists you tidy your bedroom. You ask her if you can do it later, but she says, "No! Do it now!" Then she turns off the TV. You feel yourself starting to get angry. ________________________________
7. Your classmates in Primary are messing around and your teacher looks close to tears. ________________________________
8. Your mom and dad have kissed you good night, and you notice that they have forgotten to remind you to say your prayers. You are tucked in and reading a great book. ________________________________
9. You watched the news, and some things you saw have really unsettled you. You lie in bed worrying and start to feel scared. ________________________________

All these are decisions that many of us may face often. We may not realize it, but the way we react to these and other experiences shows Heavenly Father and Jesus whether we are keeping our promises. Each good decision helps us to get better at feeling the Holy Ghost.

BAPTISM COLORING PAGE

All of the Godhead were there when Jesus was baptized. Heavenly Father's voice was heard introducing His Son, Jesus Christ, saying, "This is my beloved Son: hear Him." The Holy Ghost came down in the form of a dove.

PLAN OF HAPPINESS

Heavenly Father has a wonderful plan for us to be happy and return to Him. THE HOLY GHOST IS THERE TO HELP US EVERY STEP OF THE WAY!

PRE-EARTH LIFE We lived with Heavenly Father as spirits before we were born on earth. He told us about His plan to come to earth, and we were excited!

OUR LIFE ON EARTH We came to earth to get bodies, to make covenants, and to try to learn to be like Heavenly Father. Heavenly Father wanted to help us as much as possible, so He gave us the Holy Ghost to help, comfort, and guide us through our whole lives!

CELESTIAL KINGDOM After our earth life, we want to live with Heavenly Father and our families in the celestial kingdom. The Holy Ghost can help us live righteously and help us repent through Christ's Atonement, so we can live in eternal happiness!

Celestial Kingdom

Draw your family.

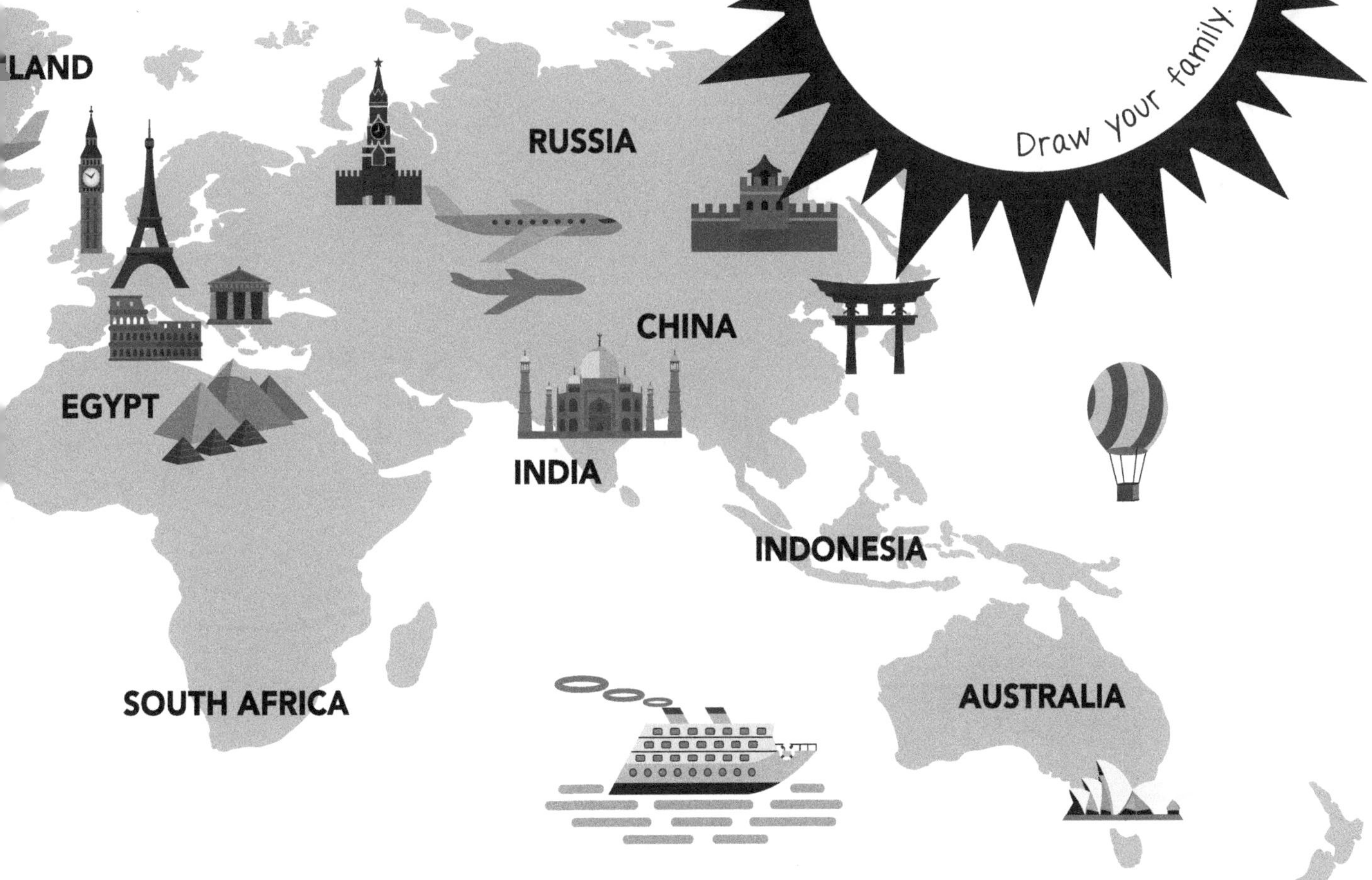

LAND

RUSSIA

CHINA

EGYPT

INDIA

INDONESIA

SOUTH AFRICA

AUSTRALIA

Mark where you live.
You can also mark any places you have traveled to.

Can you finish this picture by adding more sheep?

Who is the Holy Ghost?

THE HOLY GHOST is a member of the Godhead. Heavenly Father and Jesus are also part of the Godhead. Together, they preside over EVERYTHING! They work perfectly together, but they also have different roles. See if you can match up the member of the Godhead with the correct fact. Write the number listed by the name on the correct lines below.

1 Heavenly Father | **2 Jesus Christ** | **3 Holy Ghost** | **4 All three**

___ Created the world
___ We are created in His image
___ Does not have a body
___ Presides over all creation
___ Work together in perfect union
___ Testifies of God and Christ
___ Father of our spirits
___ Atoned for us
___ We receive revelations through Him

Expert Tip: "The most powerful Being in the universe is the Father of your spirit. He knows you. He loves you with a perfect love." Dieter F. Uchtdorf, "You Matter to Him," *Ensign*, Nov. 2011.

Word Wheel: How many words can you make that are at least two letters long that all use the center letter, "O." One word uses all 9 letters. (Hint: The theme is "The Holy Ghost.")

___________________ ___________________
___________________ ___________________
___________________ ___________________
___________________ ___________________
___________________ ___________________

C R E F O T R M (center: O)

Answer Key: 2 1 3 1 4 3 1 2 3

THE HOLY GHOST has lots of names. How many have you heard before? Here are some of the Holy Ghost's names used in the scriptures—but all the vowels have been taken out!

Fill in the blanks with the correct vowels to discover the answers.

H_ly Sp_r_t

Sp_r_t _f G_d

Sp_r_t _f th_ L_rd

C_mf_rt_r

St_ll, sm_ll v__c_

H_ly Sp_r_t _f Pr_m_s_

W X S E E T A N O E P E L D T
E I G A L E W S Z N N H Q T E
T D U S N A K X E M D L M J P
M C I P G C S H D D O M P Z D
F O D R T H T Y N N A C D S E
T M E O E G U I I H Z N W D F
R F M T N C M E F S O A H P O
N O Y E M E T I T Y F E S E M
T R R C R W E B I E E F O L O
E T E T D A V E M O S B S N C
S E H V A R T R J F X F U P Q
T H T E E N X R P I C B E A K
I H I F E A E O Y L A T L E T
F R M M N P L N T A S J A S A
Y S H E N A S Q F E M I R T E

WORD SEARCH

The Holy Ghost can help us in so many ways. As a member of the Godhead, He has been given many powers that bless our lives. This word search is full of ways the Holy Ghost can help us. See how many can you find.

COMFORT
WARN
STRENGTHEN
DIRECT
TESTIFY
REVEAL
GUIDE
TEACH
PROTECT
REMIND
SANCTIFY

See back of book for answers.

THE HOLY GHOST GUIDES

You have lots of choices to make in your life: picking good activities, deciding how you treat others, choosing what sort of media you view. Sometimes it is hard to know what the right thing is to do. The Holy Ghost is there to help you with all your choices! He can guide you to make good choices, like being baptized or saying your prayers, or He can guide you to avoid bad choices, like hitting your sister or disobeying your mom. He can guide you to serve someone, to find something you've lost, or to turn off a bad TV show. He is always there to guide you if you will listen to the thoughts and feelings He gives you to choose the right.

THE HOLY GHOST IS LIKE THE LIAHONA

Lehi and his family lived in tents in the wilderness.

One night, Heavenly Father told Lehi that they needed to travel to the Promised Land.

When Lehi woke up, he found a special compass outside his tent. It was called a Liahona.

The Liahona led Lehi's family on the best route through the wilderness and helped them find food.

The Liahona stopped working if the family didn't have faith or were mean to each other.

When they repented, it started to work again.

DOT-TO-DOT LIAHONA

Start on 1 and connect all the dots of the numbers up to 73.

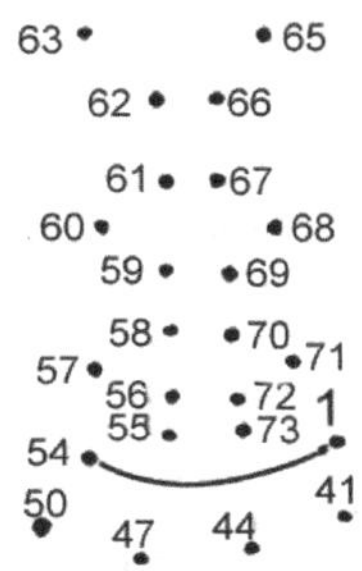
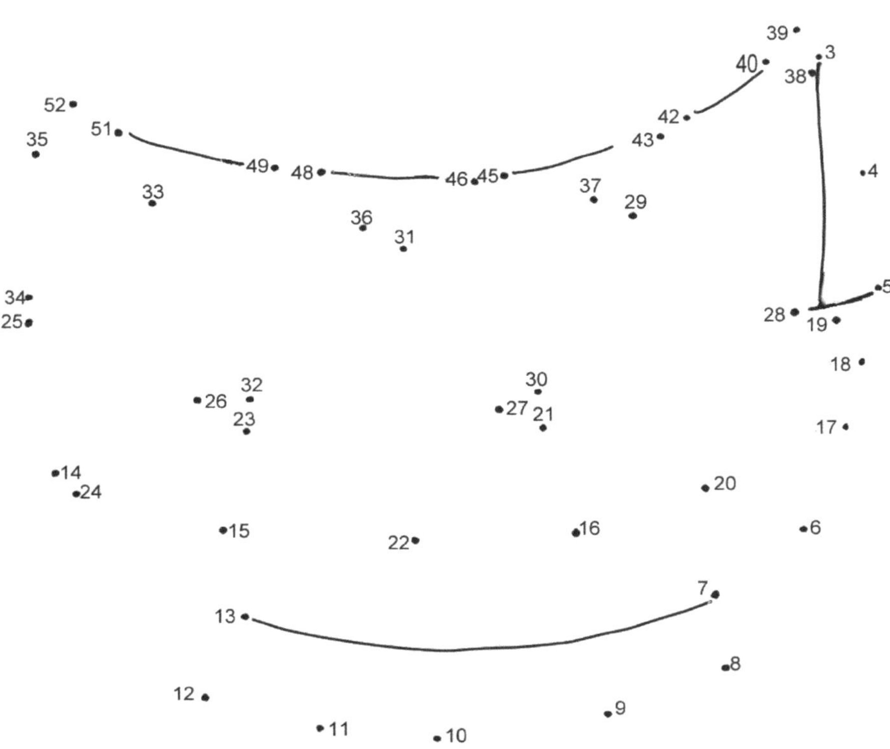

Expert Tip: "You must realize that you have something like the compass, like the Liahona, in your own system. Every child is given it. When he is eight years of age, he knows good from evil." Spencer W. Kimball, "Our Own Liahona," *Ensign*, Nov. 1976.

Instead of a Liahona, Heavenly Father has given us the gift of the Holy Ghost! It works in almost the same way. The Holy Ghost guides us and helps us find the best route through our life. The Holy Ghost doesn't work well if we sin and make bad choices, but when we repent, He can guide us again.

AMAZING!

Look at the maze on the next page. You could try to get through it without any help, but odds are that you will make some wrong turns and maybe even get a bit lost. But if you follow the clues, you can easily find your way to the end. Our life is like a maze—there are so many choices we have to make that sometimes it seems a little confusing and we might make wrong choices or feel lost. The Holy Ghost can guide us so we can make the best choices!

Expert Tip: "We may not see angels, hear heavenly voices, or receive overwhelming spiritual impressions. We frequently may press forward hoping and praying—but without absolute assurance—that we are acting in accordance with God's will. But as we honor our covenants and keep the commandments, as we strive ever more consistently to do good and to become better, we can walk with the confidence that God will guide our steps." David A. Bednar, "The Spirit of Revelation," *Ensign*, May 2011.

Promptings are like a map to help you to your destination. You choose whether to follow them.

Can you follow directions?

Activity: Create an obstacle course with chairs. Blindfold one family member or friend. Pick someone else to be the "still, small voice" that guides them through the obstacle.

WORK OUT THE SCRIPTURE CLUES THEN USE THEIR DIRECTIONS TO GET THROUGH THE MAZE!

Each scripture contains a direction (north, east, south, or west). Each time you reach a dot in the maze, follow the next direction from the scripture clues. (Hint: You won't pass all the dots if you follow the correct instructions.)

1. 2 Nephi 24:13 ______________
2. Alma 2:34 ______________
3. 1 Nephi 17:1 ______________
4. Alma 8:3 ______________
5. Omni 1:22 ______________
6. Mosiah 7:31 ______________
7. Ether 9:31 ______________
8. Alma 42:2 ______________
9. Mormon 2:6 ______________

Oh, no! Jacob has noticed the time! It's almost time to leave for church and he can't find his things (and he's still in his pajamas). Can you help him spot these hidden items? **2 shoes, pencil, ring-bound notebook, drink bottle, scripture case, 2 gloves, tie, hat, book, CTR ring**

See back of book for answers.

One of the main things that the Holy Ghost can guide you to do is serve others. If you have a thought or a feeling to do something nice, that is probably the Holy Ghost prompting you! Maybe you have had a thought to go talk to a child who looks alone, or to help your dad with the dishes, or to write a thank-you note to a teacher. Try to follow those thoughts or feelings, because that is the Holy Ghost guiding you!

Write down something nice you did for someone every day on this service calendar:

Monday	Tuesday	Wednesday	Thursday	Friday	Saturday	Sunday

At the end of the week, write a few sentences about how doing service made you feel.

____

____

Write a poem about ways the Holy Ghost could guide you to serve. For every letter, think of a way to serve. (Example: For "S," you could write "Saying thank you.")

S ______________
E ______________
R ______________
V ______________
E ______________

O ______________
T ______________
H ______________
E ______________
R ______________
S ______________

THE HOLY GHOST COMFORTS

Sad and hard things happen to all of us. At times we feel scared, lonely, uncertain, or unhappy. But Heavenly Father sent us the Holy Ghost to help us get through these times and feel comforted. It's important to remember that Heavenly Father and the Holy Ghost don't always make these hard things go away. But the Holy Ghost can help us to know that we are loved, to feel peace that Heavenly Father has a plan for us, and to cope with these hard things.

If you get a cut or scratch, you may put on a bandage to protect the wound and help it recover. The Holy Ghost can be like a bandage for us; when we are hurting emotionally or spiritually, he can help us feel better. We might need comfort when . . .

"A few years ago I had to go to the hospital for some horrible tests because I have a kidney disease. I was so frightened that I started to scream and couldn't stop. Later, when we got home, almost immediately the doctors phoned to say they were concerned and I had to go back to hospital. I was so scared and upset that I hid under the table. Mum and I said a prayer and I immediately felt calm. I was able to go back to the hospital without being scared and was able to face everything I had to have done."

Eve, age 12, Wales, UK

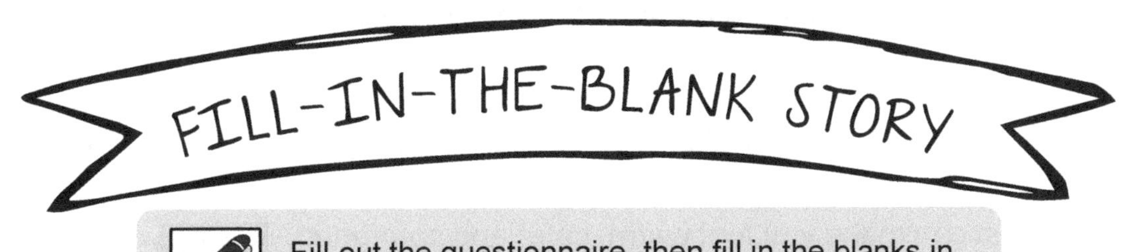

Fill out the questionnaire, then fill in the blanks in the story below with your answers to the questions.

1. Your name: ______________________

2. Item/animal you are scared of: ______________________

3. Action when you are scared: ______________________

4. A friend's name: ______________________

5. A silly name: ______________________

6. Favorite place: ______________________

7. Favorite food: ______________________

8. Three things you are grateful for:

a. ________________ b. ________________ c. ________________

9. Happy feeling: ______________________

10. Favorite activity: ______________________

1) ________ sees a 2) ________ and 3) __________. 4) ________ laughs at you and calls you a 5) _______. You try to laugh too, but you still feel jumpy and scared. You go to 6) ________ hoping that will help you calm down, but it only helps a little. You eat 7) _______ hoping it will make you feel happier, but it doesn't really help. You decide to pray. You thank Heavenly Father for 8a) ___________, 8b) ______________, and 8c) _________, then ask for the Holy Ghost to comfort you and help you not feel scared anymore. You feel 9) _______. You can now go 10) ________ without feeling scared anymore.

THE HOLY GHOST IS LIKE A BLANKET

The Holy Ghost can make you feel warm, safe, and comforted. To stay wrapped in his warmth and love, you need to do those things that keep the Spirit with you.

HOLY GHOST BLANKET GAME

YOU WILL NEED:

- 10–15 counters for every player (coins, cereal, etc.) to be used as "comfort counters"
- 1 game token per player (a colored piece of paper or game piece)
- 1 die

Place tokens on the start square. Everyone starts with 5 comfort counters. Take turns rolling a die. Every square on the blanket board will tell you to either add or take away comfort counters. The person with the most comfort counters at the end of the game wins. You can't go below 0 comfort counters.

Expert Tip: "During times of trouble or despair or simply when we need to know that God is near, the Holy Ghost can lift our spirits, give us hope, and teach us the 'peaceable things of the kingdom,' helping us feel 'the peace of God, which passeth all understanding." Craig C. Christensen, "An Unspeakable Gift from God," *Ensign*, Nov. 2012.

START

Read your scriptures.

+2 COMFORT

See a scary war on the news.

-1 COMFORT
(Go back to Start)

Have family home evening.

+3 COMFORT

Pray thoughtfully and feel peace.

+3 COMFORT

You are really stressed about a test at school.

-1 COMFORT
(Go back to Start)

An older sibling has stopped going to church, and you are worried for them.

-2 COMFORT

Get a hug from a family member.

+1 COMFORT

Watch general conference.

+2 COMFORT

Grandma is really sick.

-3 COMFORT

Some kids make fun of you on the way to school.

-2 COMFORT
(Go back to Start)

Attend Primary and sacrament meeting.

+2 COMFORT

Share your testimony with your family.

+2 COMFORT

Sing songs about Jesus.

+1 COMFORT

Fight with your friend.

-2 COMFORT
(Go back to Start)

END
The Holy Ghost is like a comforting blanket!

+3 COMFORT

You may have to go through lots of hard situations, and you will need the Holy Ghost to help and comfort you. Hard situations might include difficult school work or chores, mean bullies, lack of money, the death of a family member or friend, or wars and scary things in the world around you. People in the scriptures had to go through all these things too. By reading their stories we can see how they used the Holy Ghost to help them get through those hard times.

Match the pictures on this page with the story on the next page.

A

B

C

D

E

Answer Key: A-3, B-4, C-2, D-5, E-1

1

Nephi's brothers Laman and Lemuel bullied him. They beat him up, called him names, even threatened to kill him. Nephi always had the Spirit with him to comfort him, to help him feel positive, and to keep his self-worth, even when they were being mean (1 Nephi 7 & 18).

2

Alma and his people were trapped by the Lamanites and forced to do all the Lamanites' work. They had to do hard tasks and chores. They also were bullied because they believed in God. The Holy Ghost comforted them. He didn't take away their burdens right away, but he helped make the people stronger and helped them not feel the heavy loads (Mosiah 24).

3

Alma and Amulek taught a group of people who didn't have much money. Others left them out and were mean to them because they were poor. When Alma and Amulek taught these people the gospel, they felt the Spirit and realized that Heavenly Father thought they were important. They were so comforted that they stopped caring what the mean people thought and cared instead what Heavenly Father thought of them (Alma 32).

4

Nephi and his family were all very sad when their father, Lehi, died. Nephi's brothers Laman and Lemuel were angry that life was sad and hard. Nephi was sad, but he was able to feel peace and rejoice because the Holy Ghost helped him know God has a plan for everyone (2 Nephi 4).

5

In Helaman's time, there were 2,000 young boys who were surrounded by wars and fighting. It was very scary, especially when their families were about to be attacked and their homes destroyed. They chose to fight to save their families. God helped them feel calm, remember the teachings of their mothers, and be comforted. He also protected them (Alma 53 & 56).

THE HOLY GHOST WARNS & PROTECTS

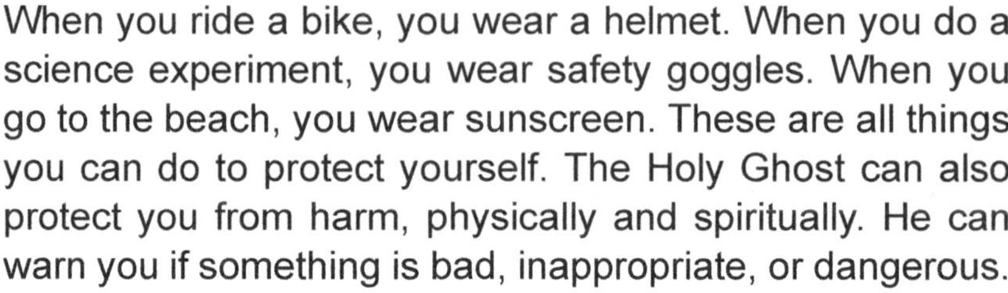

When you ride a bike, you wear a helmet. When you do a science experiment, you wear safety goggles. When you go to the beach, you wear sunscreen. These are all things you can do to protect yourself. The Holy Ghost can also protect you from harm, physically and spiritually. He can warn you if something is bad, inappropriate, or dangerous.

Crack this code to figure out what the secret message says! The code is on the next page.

      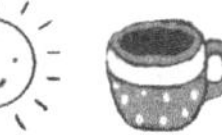 

___ ___ ___   ___ ___ ___ ___   ___ ___ ___ ___ ___

___ ___ ___   ___ ___ ___ ___ ___ ___ ___   ___ ___ ___

   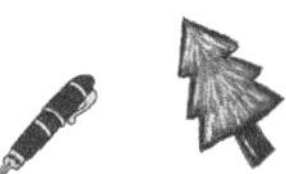  

___ ___ ___ ___   ___ ___ ___ ___

___ ___ ___   ___ ___ ___ ___ ___ ___ .

Answer Key: The Holy Ghost can protect you from harm and danger.

THE HOLY GHOST IS OUR ARMOR

If we have the Holy Ghost in our lives, it is like wearing A SPIRITUAL SUIT OF ARMOR. It can block temptations and bad influences and warn US of danger.

SWORD: Helps you fight against evil influences that attack us every day.

HELMET: Protects you from inappropriate thoughts and inappropriate things you might see or hear.

BREASTPLATE: Protects your feelings from anger, envy, hate, and other negative feelings.

SHIELD: Blocks negative outside influences, like media, gossip, or false knowledge, so it won't hurt or confuse you.

BOOTS: Helps you want to walk in good and holy places and to stand up for righteousness.

Expert Tip: "Choose wisely when using media because whatever you read, listen to, or look at has an effect on you. Select only media that uplifts you." *For the Strength of Youth*, (2011), 11.

THE HOLY GHOST HELPS YOU AVOID BAD INFLUENCES

A BOAT IS SURROUNDED BY WATER, but it will stay afloat as long as the water doesn't get INSIDE the boat. Our lives are like a boat. You can stay happy and afloat in the gospel, even though you are surrounded by lots of evils in the world, as long as you don't let bad influences into your life. If you let too much darkness in, your testimony might start to "sink." The Holy Ghost helps you know what is good and what is bad, so you can let only good things in.

Nephi and his family were traveling to the promised land on a boat. Laman and Lemuel and others in their family started to do bad things. They sang and danced to songs that didn't bring the Spirit, and they said bad and mean things. Their compass, the Liahona, stopped working, so they didn't know the way, and their boat almost sank in a storm (1 Nephi 18:8–12).

Make a boat like Nephi's to remind you to keep out the bad influences and choices from your life so you stay afloat.

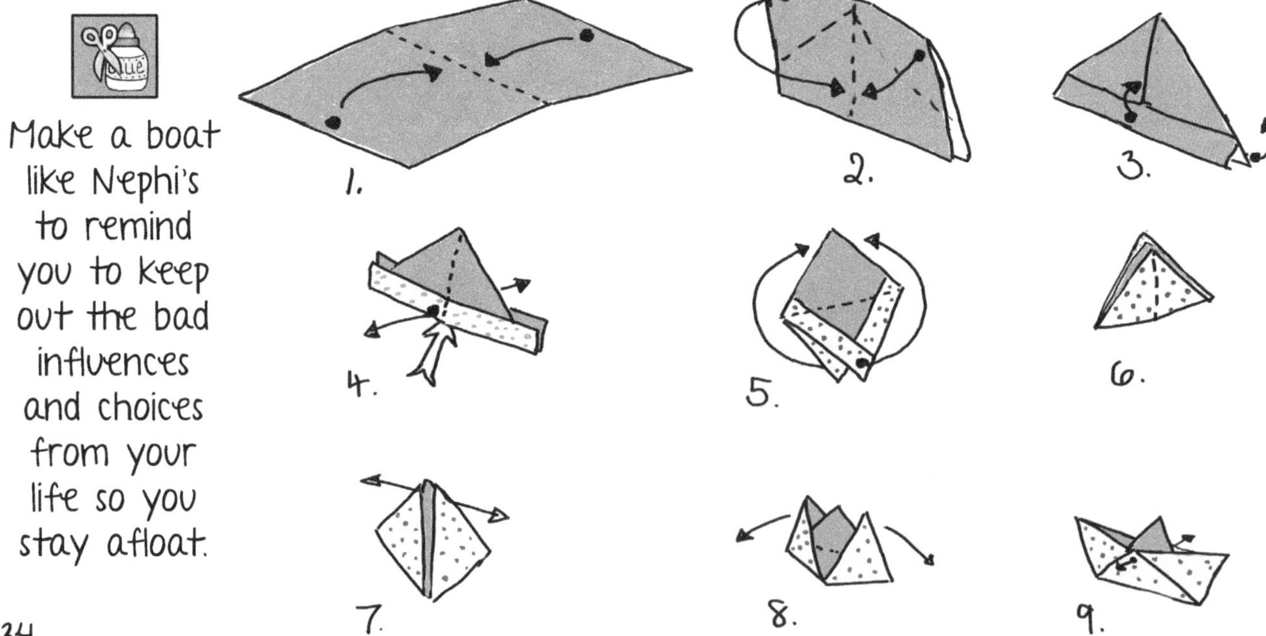

STAYING ON THE SAFE PATH GAME

The Holy Ghost helps us stay on the safest path through life. If we leave the safe path of the gospel standards, it is hard for the Holy Ghost to protect us.

INSTRUCTIONS: Try to stay on the safe gospel path, away from dangers and temptations!

NEED: Ballpoint pens

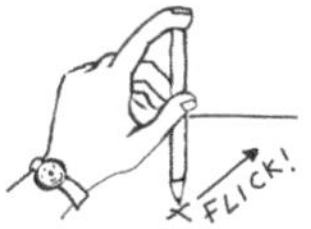

FLICK!

Player 1, place the tip of the pen at the start with a finger on the pen end. Push down on the end of the pen to make the pen flick forward, hopefully leaving a line. Where the pen line ends is your starting point for next time. Everyone take a turn. Then Player 1 flicks from his or her "end spot." Try to get around the route first. If you stray off the path and hit an obstacle off the path, you lose a turn!

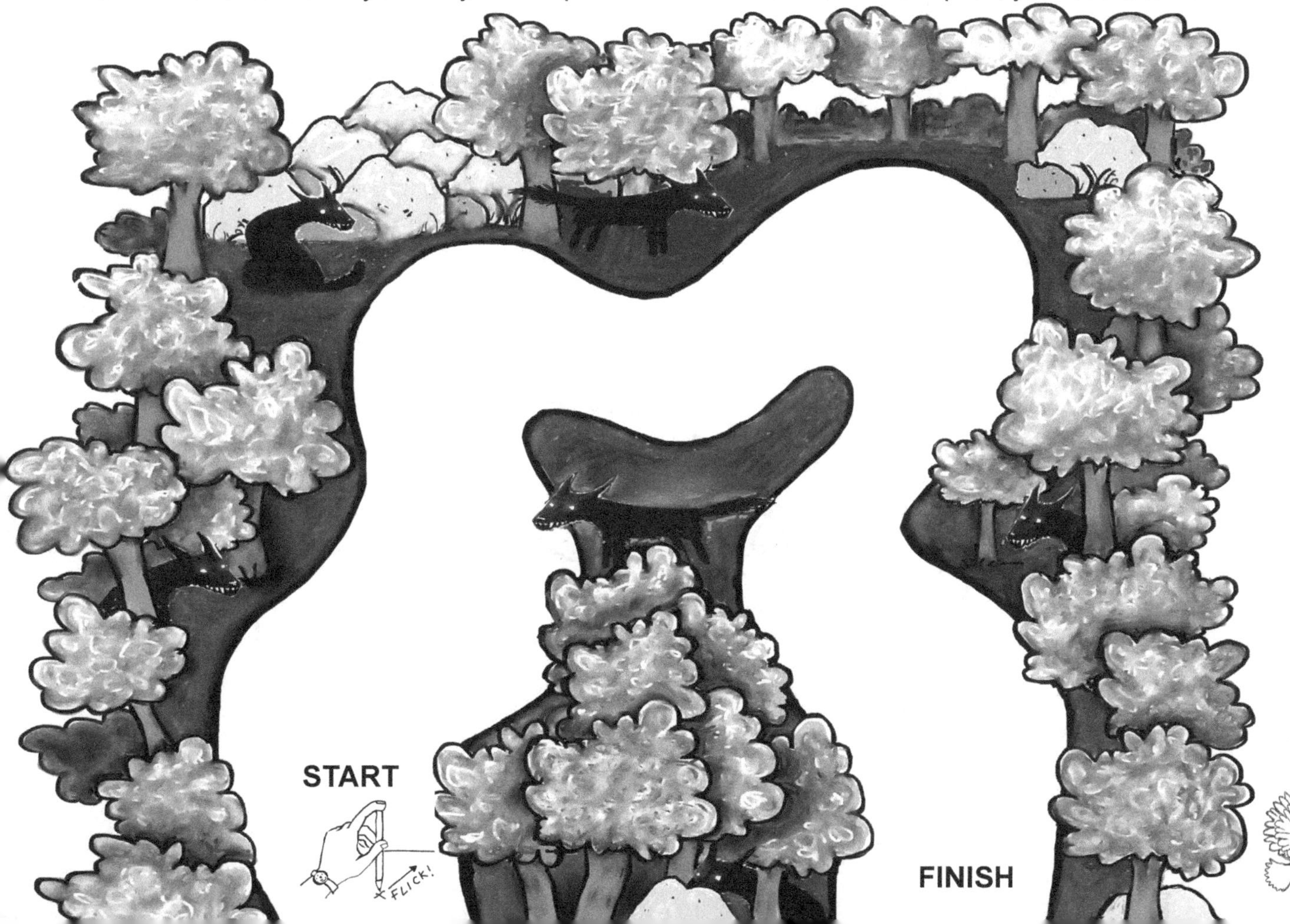

START

FLICK!

FINISH

THE HOLY GHOST TESTIFIES & TEACHES

Another responsibility of the Holy Ghost is to TESTIFY and TEACH you what is true. The Holy Ghost helps you gain a testimony of important things. For instance, when your teacher bears her testimony of Jesus Christ, you might feel a warm, happy feeling from the Holy Ghost telling you what your teacher says is true. The Holy Ghost can help you understand the scriptures or gospel principles by putting thoughts into your head of what something means. He can also remind you of things you've already learned, like reminding you of the facts you've studied for a test. The Holy Ghost speaks to your mind and your heart to help you learn important things.

Sometimes you might not realize you have a testimony until you bear it. When you testify of Christ, the Holy Ghost can help you know what you are saying is true.

HERE ARE SOME VITAL THINGS YOU NEED TO GAIN A TESTIMONY OF.

FOLLOW THE LINES TO THE ANSWERS.

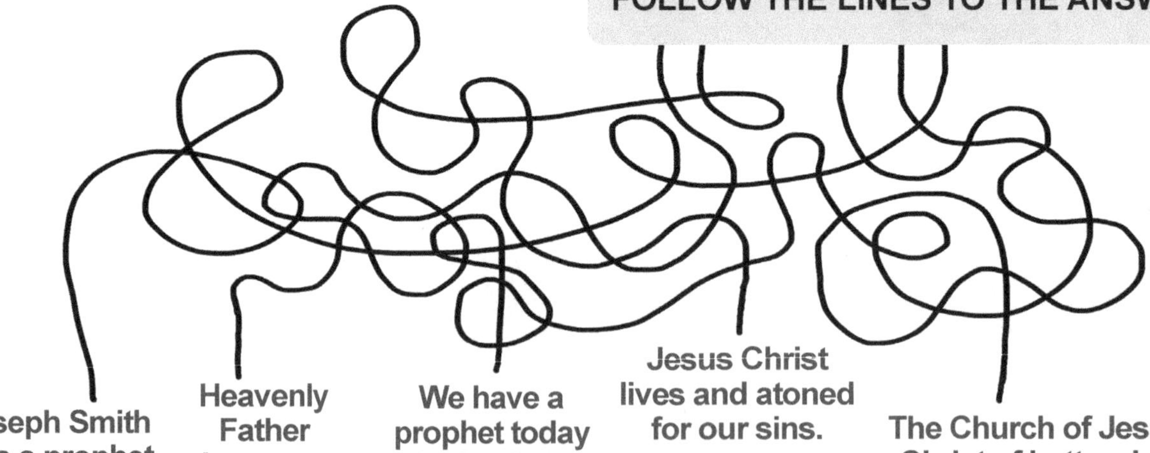

Joseph Smith was a prophet who restored the Church.

Heavenly Father loves us.

We have a prophet today who leads our Church.

Jesus Christ lives and atoned for our sins.

The Church of Jesus Christ of Latter-day Saints is God's true church on the earth.

YOUR TESTIMONY

WRITE YOUR TESTIMONY

Finish the picture above.

Activity: Bear your testimony at church or to a friend. Pay attention to how you feel. Does it make you feel good? Warm? Peaceful? The Holy Ghost will testify to you when you or others speak truth. When you bear your testimony about Heavenly Father, Jesus, and the restored gospel, He can let you know you are saying the right things.

Expert Tip: "We become taller in testimony like we grow taller in physical stature; we hardly know it happens because it comes by growth." Boyd K. Packer, "The Quest for Spiritual Knowledge," *New Era*, Jan. 2007.

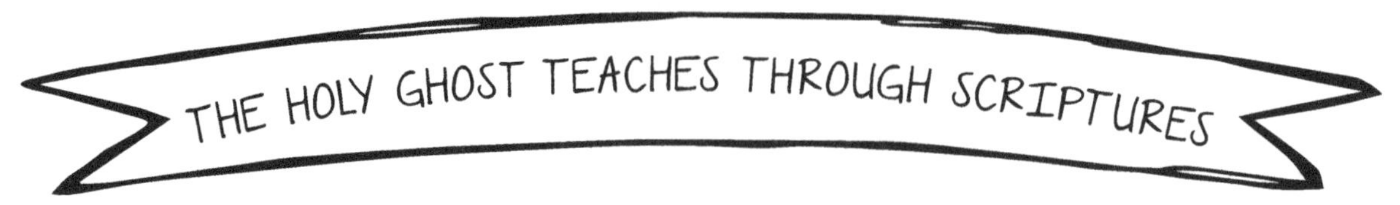

One of the very best ways to learn about eternal truths is from the SCRIPTURES. The Holy Ghost testifies that what you read in the scriptures is true. Even though the scriptures can be hard to understand, the Holy Ghost can help you start to figure them out. He often answers prayers through the verses and stories you read in the scriptures. For instance, if you are feeling sad, maybe you'll read a verse about comfort.

Here's a scripture challenge for you! Try to read at least a few scripture verses every day. Here is a list of scriptures about the Holy Ghost. Every day that you read at least one verse, color in part of the picture.

1) Moroni 10:4–5
2) 2 Nephi 32:5
3) D&C 45:57
4) Moses 5:58
5) Galatians 5:22–23
6) Romans 5:5
7) 2 Nephi 31:12
8) Moses 6:61
9) John 14:26
10) 1 Corinthians 2:9–10
11) Acts 2:38
12) D&C 11:12–14
13) Moroni 8:26
14) Alma 9:21
15) Matthew 28:19
16) D&C 8:2
17) Alma 5:45–46
18) D&C 31:11
19) 1 Nephi 4:6
20) 1 Corinthians 6:19
21) Acts 5:32
22) Helaman 5:45
23) Matthew 3:16
24) D&C 130:22
25) 2 Nephi 33:1–2
26) Moses 6:52
27) 1 Nephi 10:19
28) Alma 17:10
29) John 15:26
30) John 14:16–17
31) D&C 42:17

It can be hard to get into reading the scriptures, so here are some tips . . .

- Read scriptures with a parent so they can explain some of the words you don't understand.
- Ask your parents or teachers to help you find the chapters with your favorite scripture heroes.
- Pick just a few verses every day.
- Read a scripture story in the Book of Mormon reader, then read the same story in the scriptures.
- Draw a picture or comic of what you are reading about.
- Memorize a scripture verse.

HOLY
GHOST
1
2
3
4
5
6
7
8
9
10
11
12
13
14
15
16
17
18
19
20
21
22
23
24
25
26
27
28
29
30
31

Some places are better for FEELING THE SPIRIT than others. The best places are "holy places" like the temple, your home, or your church. If a place is too noisy or busy, or has negative influences, it can block the Spirit. There are also many things that can help bring the Spirit, such as scriptures, pictures of Christ, and sacred music.

Activity: This board is full of places and things that can help invite the Holy Ghost into your life. Color in the pictures of things you have used, places you have visited, or things you have done.

Optional Game: Place a small treat or snack on each image. One person leaves the room while the rest pick one image as "special." When the person comes back into the room, they eat one treat at a time until they pick up the treat on the "special" spot. Then they have to stop picking treats and their turn is over.

When you know lots of Primary songs, the Holy Ghost can put a song in your head to guide, remind, comfort, or teach you. For this game, divide into two teams. Pick one of the themes below (or make up your own). For each theme, each team takes turns singing a primary song that relates to that theme. The other team has to think of another song in that theme before the singing team has finished singing the song, otherwise the team singing wins the round.

THEMES:

- Jesus Christ
- Baptism
- Scriptures
- Christmas
- Prophets
- Family
- Gratitude
- Prayer
- Happiness
- Reverence
- Choosing the right

Expert Tip: "The Holy Ghost can bring all things to their remembrance, but the words of SCRIPTURES and HYMNS will last the longest." Henry B. Eyring, "A Priceless Heritage of Hope," *Ensign*, May 2014 (emphasis added).

TEST YOUR GOSPEL KNOWLEDGE!

1. Who baptized Jesus? (Matthew 3:13) ________________
2. How old was Joseph Smith when he prayed in the Sacred Grove and saw Heavenly Father and Jesus? (JS–H 1:16–17, 23) ______
3. Which prophet taught the gospel before being burned by wicked King Noah? (Mosiah 11:26–27, 17:20) ______________
4. How many Articles of Faith are there? ______
5. Which prophet was given the Ten Commandments and parted the Red Sea? (1 Nephi 4:2, Deuteronomy 10:4) _______________
6. What is the first book in the Book of Mormon? ___________
7. Which prophet built an ark and filled it with animals? (Genesis 7:12–16) _____________________
8. Who translated the Book of Mormon? (Book of Mormon Introduction) _____________________

See back of book for answers.

"The Primary was invited to sing 'I Wonder When He Comes Again' in sacrament meeting. I remember standing up in front on the stand and as we sang:

I'm sure he'll call his little ones
Together 'round his knee,
Because he said in days gone by,
'Suffer them to come to me.'

My heart felt such a warm, loving hug surrounding me testifying that God loves me and He knows me. The joy I felt made me smile inside and out."

Becky, age 8, Utah, USA

THE HOLY GHOST SANCTIFIES

The Holy Ghost can change us and help us become more like Heavenly Father. He is like a gardener for our lives. He not only helps us pull out all the weeds (prompts us to repent and not do bad things), but he helps us plant flowers (helps us become more Christlike). For example, the Holy Ghost may tell you to repent after being mean to your sister and also prompt you on how you could be more loving toward her in the future. Under all the weeds, write an activity or attribute you feel you should “weed out” of your life. Under all the flowers, write an activity or attribute that you would like to “plant” in your life to help you become more Christlike.

Expert Tip: "If you have felt the influence of the Holy Ghost [today], you may take it as evidence that the Atonement is working in your life. For that reason and many others, you would do well to put yourself in places and in tasks that invite the promptings of the Holy Ghost. . . . The reception of the Holy Ghost cleanses us through the Atonement of Jesus Christ." Henry B. Eyring, "Gifts of the Spirit for Hard Times" (Church Education Fireside, September 10, 2006), speeches.byu.edu.

Color these pages and add more bugs.

REPENTANCE

The Holy Ghost can help you know when you're doing wrong and need to REPENT. You might think guilt is a bad thing, but the Holy Ghost helps you feel guilty so you can know a behavior is wrong and help you want to change. It's actually a blessing because it's like having a kind friend who lets you know when you're headed the wrong way.

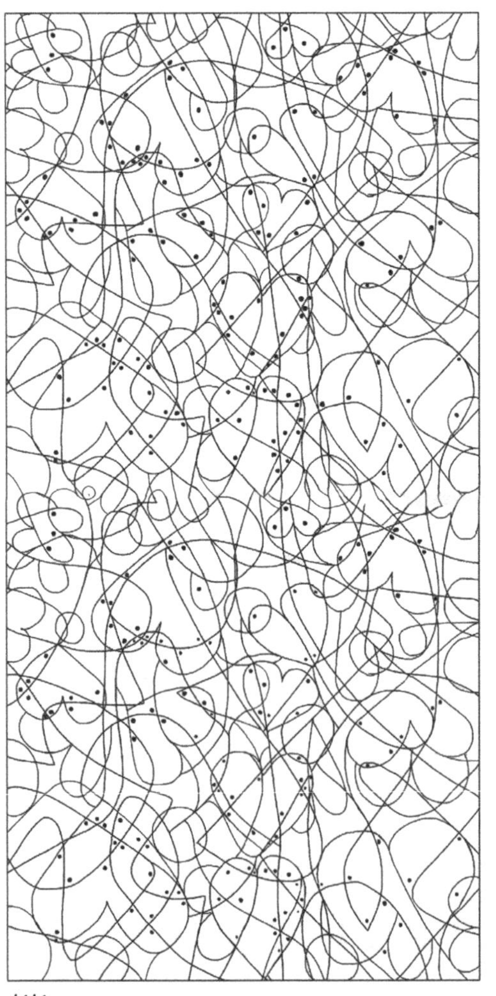

Sin can keep the Holy Ghost from communicating with and helping us. Unfortunately, everyone (except Jesus) sins, even if we are trying really hard to be good. It's part of being human. But through the Atonement, we can be forgiven. Jesus atoned for everyone, including you, in the Garden of Gethsemane, and the Holy Ghost brings that cleansing power into your life. When you repent, the Holy Ghost makes you clean again, through the Atonement.

Find and color the sections with a dot in them to uncover the hidden hearts. How many are there?

MIGHTY CHANGE OF HEART

Alma taught about having a "mighty change of heart" (Alma 5). A mighty change of heart is when someone is truly converted to the gospel and changes to be better. After King Benjamin's people listened to him teach, they had a mighty change of heart and they didn't want to do bad things anymore—only good. If your heart wants to do good things all day long, you know you've had a mighty change of heart. The Holy Ghost can help your heart change.

Answer: 26

The Holy Ghost will help CHANGE us, but we have to be striving to improve for that change to happen. We need to be aware of our weaknesses for them to be made strong. We need the desire to change. The Holy Ghost can help us honestly analyze how we are doing—our weaknesses AND our strengths. If you don't do very well at something, you know where you can start improving!

Write the number that matches how often you do each of these things. Where do you need to improve? What do you need to stop doing? What do you need to start doing?

1 (Always) 2 (Usually) 3 (Sometimes) 4 (Rarely) 5 (Never)

Do I:

___ Say thoughtful prayers

___ Pay tithing on any money received

___ Act reverently during the sacrament

___ Listen and participate in Primary

___ Treat others with kindness

___ Tell the truth

___ Work hard at school

___ Say sorry and repent after doing something wrong

___ Serve others

___ Express gratitude

Do I avoid:

___ Media (shows, games, music, etc.) that is violent, swears, contains nudity

___ Gossiping

___ Swearing

___ Arguing and fighting

___ Excluding or leaving someone out

___ Wearing inappropriate or immodest clothes

___ People who try to lead me astray

___ Places where it is hard to feel the Spirit

I need to . . .
Listen to the Spirit.
Draw some pictures to go with what you need to do.
I need to . . .
Can you fill in the thought bubbles with other ways you can serve?
I need to . . .

How to Use Your Gift

I need to . . .

I need to . . .

I need to . . .
serve others.

There are things you can do every day to make sure THE HOLY GHOST WORKS IN YOUR LIFE. Fill in the thumbs up if you do the spiritual activity or the thumbs down if you don't—and if you don't, you know what you can work on next to help you feel the Holy Ghost.

  Pray—morning, evening, on the food, as a family, and throughout the day

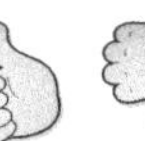  Read scriptures

  Keep commandments

  Serve others

  Have faith in Heavenly Father and Jesus Christ

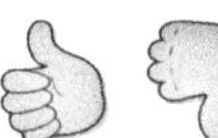 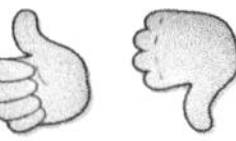 Have faith the Holy Ghost can guide you

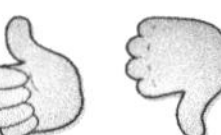  Go to church every week

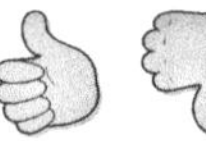 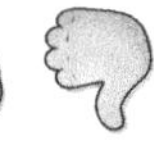 Attend church activities

  Share the gospel

SPIRIT METER:

How am I doing on feeling the Spirit today?

Empty (sad), halfway (okay), FULL (happy)?

QUICK GUIDE:
AM I FEELING THE SPIRIT?

AM I:	AM I:
• Happy	• Angry
• Peaceful	• Contentious
• Confident	• Scared
• Excited about the gospel	• Doubtful
• Eager to serve	• Easily offended
• Enlightened	• Dark
• Open and happy to be around others	• Secretive
• Happy to pray	• Not wanting to pray
• Thinking of Jesus often	• Never thinking of Jesus
= FEELING THE SPIRIT	**= NOT FEELING THE SPIRIT**

PARABLE OF THE TEN VIRGINS

There were ten ladies waiting with their oil lamps for a wedding party, but the party was late. By the time everyone arrived, five of the ladies had run out of oil for their lamps. The other five were prepared with spare oil, so they could join the party with their lit lamps. (To read the scripture story, go to Matthew 25:1–13.) Imagine the oil is like our relationship with the Holy Ghost. Unexpected and often unpleasant things happen to us, but if we keep our spiritual lamps burning brightly then we need not fear or be anxious. We'll be okay.

It takes constant work and effort to keep your light burning brightly. When you do something to invite the Spirit, or when you have a spiritual experience, you add oil to your lamp. Below, draw a drop of oil in your lamp with every spiritual experience. Label it with what you did. Try to fill the lamp with lots of spiritual oil, so that your testimony can stay burning brightly, no matter what!

Expert Tip: "Spiritual light rarely comes to those who merely sit in darkness waiting for someone to flip a switch." Dieter F. Uchtdorf, "The Hope of God's Light," *Ensign*, May 2013.

In the picture below, circle each girl who has brought some spare oil.

YOUR ROUND-THE-CLOCK FRIEND

HEAVENLY FATHER never wants you to struggle on your own and that is why he has sent you THE HOLY GHOST as your CONSTANT COMPANION. Another word for "companion" is "friend." Like any other friend, it will take some work to get to know Him and find out how He communicates. Also, like a friend, there are ways you can hurt His feelings and force Him to leave you alone. But as you get to know Him and act in a way that invites Him to stay, the Holy Ghost can be the very best friend you could ever have, 24 hours a day, 7 days a week!

ROUND THE CLOCK

7:00 Prayers asking for guidance and safety.

8:00 Missing shoe. Prompting of where it is.

9:00 Make fun of someone, but feel bac and say sorry.

10:00 Scary test, but you pray and fee calm and remember what you studied

11:00 A book you read contains swea words. You choose a different one.

12:00 Prompted to talk with a kic sitting on his own.

1:00 You feel the need to defenc the Church in class after somethinç bad is said.

2:00 A warning thought tells you tc look again as you cross the road You almost didn't see that car!

3:00 You ask a friend to turn off a violent video game because it makes you feel uncomfortable.

4:00 Your mom is cleaning up the kitchen You know you should help her so you do.

5:00 You bear your testimony in FHE lesson anc it makes you feel so good inside.

6:00 As you pray, you see so many ways you have hac the Holy Ghost with you today!

Learning to understand the Holy Ghost can be a little like LEARNING A NEW LANGUAGE. It takes a lot of patience, practice, and effort. Becoming close and responsive to the Spirit is a lifelong quest, so don't be frustrated if you don't get it all straight away. When you learn a language, you start with just a few words. When learning to understand the Holy Ghost, you can start with recognizing how you feel when the Holy Ghost is with you. Don't get frustrated when you don't know how to understand the Spirit. Just keep practicing like you would if you were learning a language.

Here, the word "prayer" is written in 8 different languages. Can you match the word with the correct language it is written in?

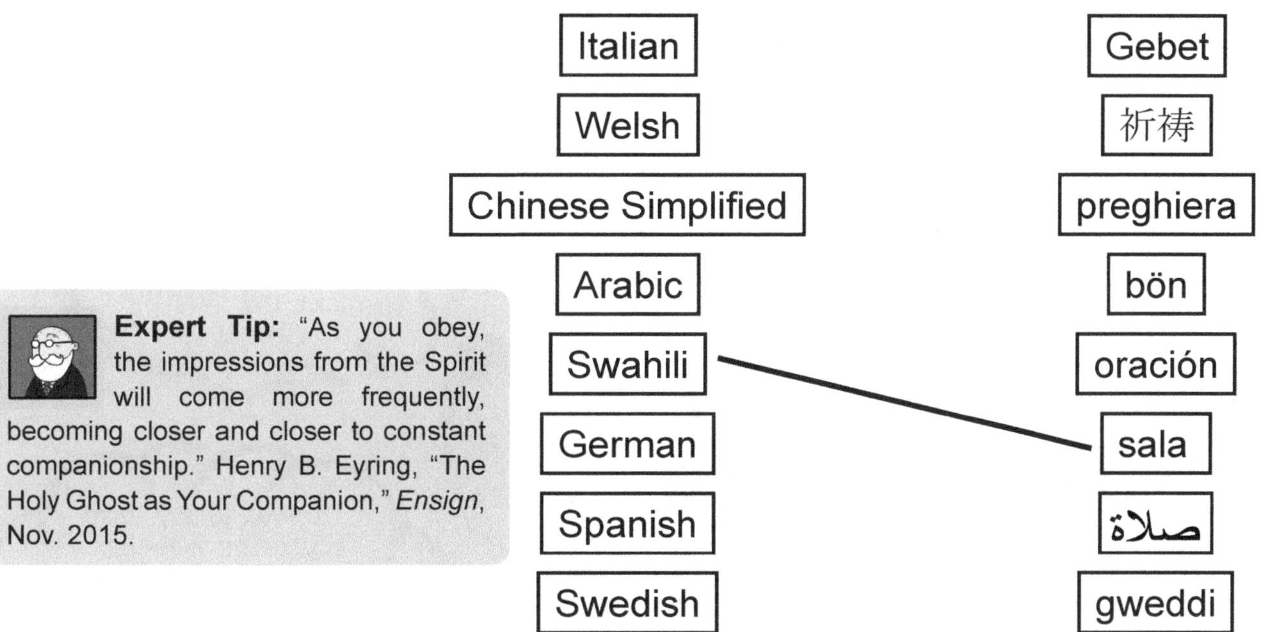

Expert Tip: "As you obey, the impressions from the Spirit will come more frequently, becoming closer and closer to constant companionship." Henry B. Eyring, "The Holy Ghost as Your Companion," *Ensign*, Nov. 2015.

Italian = preghiera, Welsh = gweddi, Chinese Simplified = 祈祷, Arabic = صلاة, Swahili = sala, German = Gebet, Spanish = oración, Swedish = bön

THOUGHTS

The Holy Ghost is often called THE "STILL, SMALL VOICE." That name might make you guess that the Holy Ghost usually talks to you in an actual voice, but that's not generally the case. Most often, the Holy Ghost communicates through thoughts and feelings. If you wait to hear an actual voice, you may not feel like the Holy Ghost is guiding you. But if you learn to listen to the thoughts and feelings that the Holy Ghost sends to you, you'll realize He is communicating with you all the time!

Look at the following thoughts Katie is having. Cross out the ones that you think are NOT promptings from the Holy Ghost. Read the rest. If you have ever had thoughts like these, you've probably felt the Holy Ghost!

I lost my favorite toy. After praying, a thought popped into my head where to look, and I found it!

The Holy Ghost often sends little thoughts into your head: an act of service you could do, a warning of something bad, a memory of where you left something, or the words from a scripture, quote, or song to help you out. These thoughts from the Holy Ghost are given to guide you every day.

I know it was wrong to say that swear word. I need to make my language cleaner.

I was angry with my sister. A memory of us playing together popped into my head and helped me get rid of the angry feelings.

Expert Tip: "The Holy Ghost communicates with our spirits through the mind more than through the physical senses." Boyd K. Packer, "Prayer and Promptings," *Ensign*, Nov. 2009.

I'll never be able to do that as well as him.

I know Heavenly Father loves me.

I learned about Joseph Smith in Primary, and I believe he is a true prophet.

A friend asked about the gospel. Suddenly I knew what to say.

I read the scriptures by myself and I understood most of what was going on, even though the words were hard.

A Primary song came into my head and helped me do the right thing.

I knew I needed to stand up against the children bullying the new kid.

I remembered my dad told me not to do that.

I studied really hard for a test. I remembered what I had studied.

I'm not good enough.

I think I should go talk to that kid who is sitting alone.

Everyone else is better than me.

I should help my mom do the dishes.

FEELINGS

Look at how David is feeling. Cross out those that are not feelings from the Holy Ghost. If you've ever felt anything like the lovely feelings that are left, you've probably felt the Holy Ghost!

The Holy Ghost sends you feelings to teach, guide, and comfort you. You might feel joy while doing something good, comfort when you need it, guilt after making mistakes, or warmth when you bear your testimony. All these feelings are straight from the Holy Ghost to help you in your life.

I don't feel like praying today.

I feel warm and peaceful when I am at church or I visit the temple.

I'm lonely and I don't feel like I'm good enough to have any friends.

When my grandma died, I felt so sad, but I was able to feel comfort and hope that I would see her again.

When I listened to general conference, I felt love toward the prophet and knew he was a prophet of God.

Expert Tip: "The Holy Ghost speaks with a voice that you *feel* more than you *hear*. . . . While we speak of 'listening' to the whisperings of the Spirit, most often one describes a spiritual prompting by saying, 'I had a *feeling* . . .'" Boyd K. Packer, "Personal Revelation: The Gift, the Test, and the Promise," *Ensign*, Nov. 1994.

My sister broke my toy and I'm feeling angry.

It was hard to fast, but it felt right.

I hurt my friend's feelings. I feel sick and worried. I know I need to say sorry.

I had a nightmare so I said a prayer. Now I don't feel scared.

I felt like I should stop by to see my friend. She was feeling sad and was grateful I had come.

I feel peace that Heavenly Father knows that I'm trying my best and that He forgives me.

I feel such love for my family and am grateful we will be a family forever.

I felt a warm tingle in my heart when I bore my testimony.

When I got lost, I prayed and felt calm. I knew I should stay where I was until my mom found me.

I felt a warning not to answer the door, so I didn't.

I saw something bad on TV. I felt sad and knew to turn it off.

I'm scared.

I spent the afternoon with my family. I feel so happy.

PRAYER is perhaps the most important aspect of REVELATION and FEELING THE HOLY GHOST. You pray to ask for the influence and guidance of the Holy Ghost. Prayer helps you feel close to Heavenly Father. During and after prayers, it is important to listen and leave time for the Holy Ghost to prompt you with thoughts and feelings.

PRAYER TIME LINE:

BEFORE: Try thinking of what you want to pray about before you begin your prayer. It helps your prayers be more focused.

AFTER: After you've finished your prayer, stay kneeling and think about how you feel. Listen and pay attention to what thoughts come into your head. If you jump straight up, you might not hear an answer you asked for.

BEFORE PRAYER — DURING PRAYER — AFTER PRAYER

DURING: Stay focused on praying and don't let your mind wander to other things, like what's for breakfast. Try not to rush. Thank Heavenly Father for blessings, ask for help and guidance with specific problems, and ask for forgiveness for mistakes.

Closing your eyes helps you not get distracted with other things.

Try saying personal prayers out loud. It can help you feel like you are really talking to Heavenly Father.

IT'S EASIEST TO FEEL THE SPIRIT WHEN YOU ARE ALONE IN A QUIET AND PEACEFUL PLACE.

Make time regularly for prayers. Don't rush them.

Folding your arms keeps hands still and helps you concentrate on the prayer.

Kneeling and bowing your head shows reverence to Heavenly Father.

PRAYER CROSSWORD

Which of these prayers are righteous in their desires?

Please! Please, help my Mommy get better soon.

I don't want to do my test tomorrow. Please can my school burn down tonight...?

Please help me to be kind to everyone today.

DOWN

1. The Lord heareth the prayer of the _______ (Proverbs 15:29)
2. We bow our heads and close our _____
3. Pray in your ________ (3 Nephi 18:21)
5. Let him ask in ______, nothing wavering (James 1:5–6)
8. Heavenly Father always ________ to our prayers

ACROSS

4. We pray to: _______
6. Hearken unto the ________ which teacheth a man to pray (2 Nephi 32:8–9)
7. _______, and it shall be given you (Matthew 7:7)
9. We pray in the name of _______ _______
10. Final word in a prayer: _______

"One day, we were driving to the park to play and have a picnic, but on the way it started to rain. Mum said we'd have to go home. I quietly said a prayer that the rain would stop for us. When we pulled up by the park, the rain stopped. It was sunny for the whole time we were at the park and the moment we got back in the car, it started to rain again. I told Mum about my prayer and we knew that my prayer had been answered."

Joseph, age 10, Wales, UK

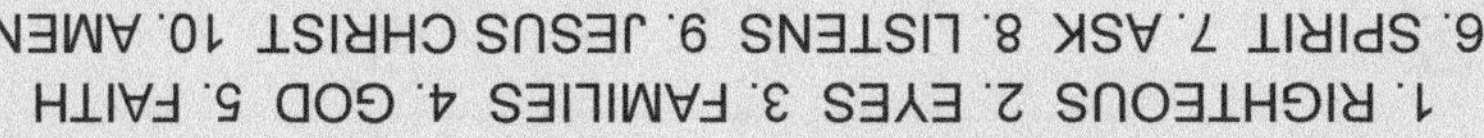

For every letter, try to think of something you could pray about that is important to you, that you need help with, or that you are grateful for. Optional: Play against a friend and see how many you can complete in 3 minutes!

A: ____________ B: ____________ C: ____________ D: ____________ E: ____________
F: ____________ G: ____________ H: ____________ I: ____________ J: ____________
K: ____________ L: ____________ M: ____________ N: ____________ O: ____________
P: ____________ Q: ____________ R: ____________ S: ____________ T: ____________
U: ____________ V: ____________ W: ____________ X: ____________ Y: ____________
Z: ____________

It would be nice to be able to text Heavenly Father, but although we don't have his number on our phone, in reality we do have direct communication with Him. We can talk to him anytime—He will never be "out of signal" or busy. Heavenly Father always has a direct line open to talk! We can block this line by sinning, being too busy, or having negative emotions like anger or envy. So try to live in such a way that you always keep communication open with Heavenly Father.

FIND THE ONLY DIRECT PHONE LINE:

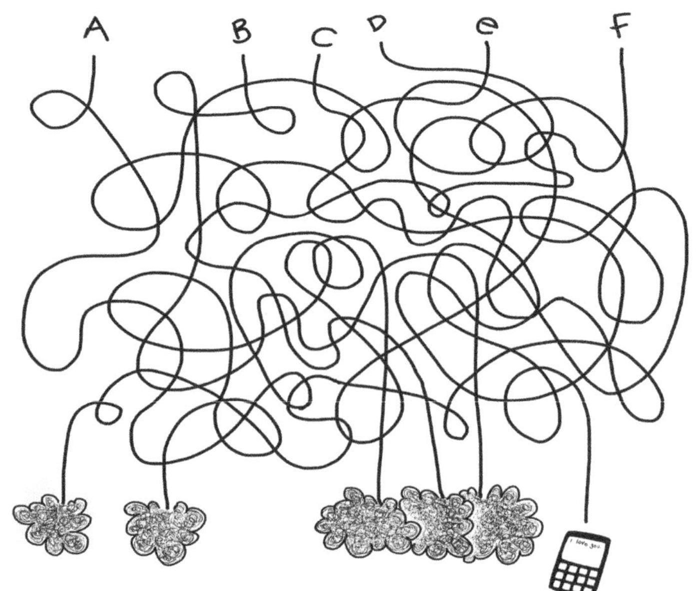

WHAT SHOULD I PRAY ABOUT?

WRITE A WISH LIST of things you'd really like for your next birthday or for Christmas.

1. ______________________ 3. ______________________

2. ______________________ 4. ______________________

Even if you asked for these things in your prayers, that wouldn't mean you'd receive all these things. A prayer should not just be our wish list of things we want from Heavenly Father. It's the other way around! It is about finding out what Heavenly Father wants for us. Heavenly Father will ALWAYS listen to our prayers, and He will ALWAYS answer. But He won't always give us what we ask for. Sometimes we ask for things that are bad for us or not right. Sometimes He has even better plans for us. When we pray, we should be asking and listening for what God's plan is, not trying to tell God what our plan is. The answer might sometimes be "no," even if we really, really want something.

Try to guess what this picture is showing. You can only see a small part of the picture, so it is hard to tell what it is. Look in the back of the book to see the full picture. Sometimes, when we ask for a blessing in prayer, we can only see a small part of our lives, so it seems like a good idea—even though we might be wrong! But Heavenly Father sees the plan for our whole life! He knows what is best for us in the long term. Trust that He knows best.

Expert Tip: "Prayer is Your personal key to heaven." Boyd K. Packer, "Personal Revelation: The Gift, the Test, and the Promise," *Ensign*, Nov. 1994.

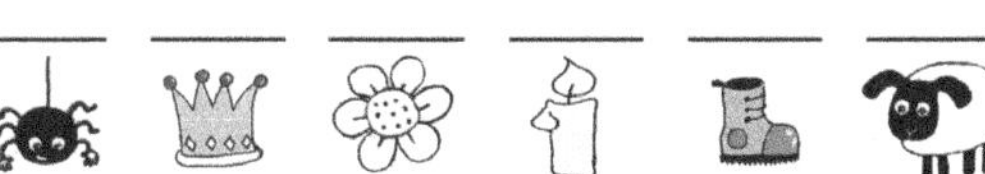

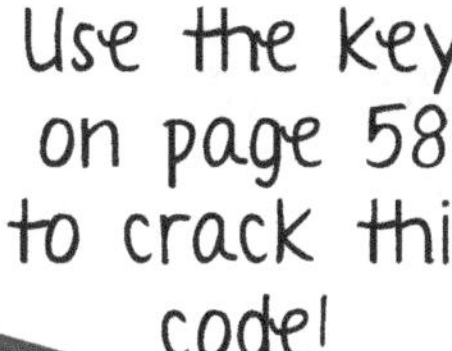
Use the key on page 58 to crack this code!

Answer Key: Heavenly Father always hears our prayers.

REVELATION is when HEAVENLY FATHER COMMUNICATES with His children—which includes you! This communication can happen in many ways, such as through scriptures, prophets, dreams, thoughts, feelings, visions, songs, and lessons. Although we might wish for Him to send the answers to our prayers straight to our minds instantly and clearly, it doesn't always work like that. Instead, we might get our answers well after we've got up from our knees: while we are listening in Primary, talking with our parents, pondering quietly, studying scriptures, or listening to general conference.

HEAVENLY FATHER SPEAKS THROUGH PROPHETS. The Lord speaks through His prophets. While you are given revelation for your specific situations and problems, prophets are given revelation for the whole Church! If you listen to the prophet, he can tell you what God wants you to know.

Can you name the prophets? These are pictures of the prophets of our dispensation.

1. **2.** **3.** **4.** **5.** **6.** **7.** **8.**

9. **10.** **11.** **12.** **13.** **14.** **15.** **16.**

1. Joseph Smith 2. Brigham Young 3. John Taylor 4. Wilford Woodruff 5. Lorenzo Snow 6. Joseph F. Smith
7. Heber J. Grant 8. George Albert Smith 9. David O. McKay 10. Joseph Fielding Smith 11. Harold B. Lee
12. Spencer W. Kimball 13. Ezra Taft Benson 14. Howard W. Hunter 15. Gordon B. Hinckley 16. Thomas S. Monson

REVELATION OFTEN COMES A SMALL PIECE AT A TIME, like putting together a puzzle. We can't pick how much revelation we will get, or when we will get it. Heavenly Father says that He gives revelation "line upon line, precept upon precept, here a little and there a little" (2 Nephi 28:30), which means piece by piece, slowly over time. In the Lord's time, He will give you everything you need to know. Often a piece of revelation might be a really small thing, like a thought to clean your room, or say something nice, or be more grateful. Don't ignore the little tiny ways to improve or serve.

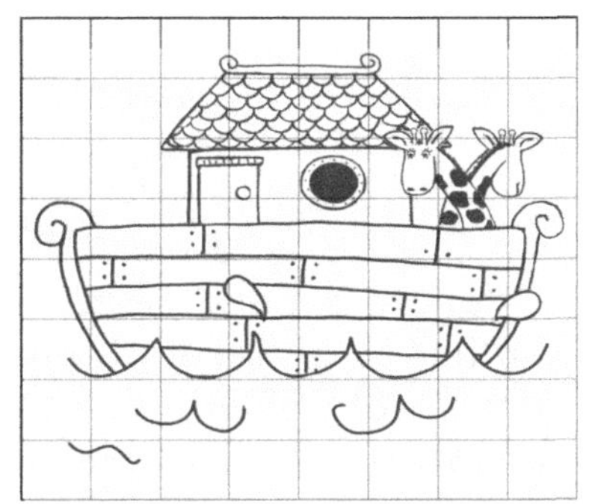

Draw the ark on the large grid, one square at a time.

Often, to get an ANSWER TO PRAYERS, you may have to do more than simply ask Heavenly Father to give you the answer. Joseph Smith taught that you should "study it out in your mind" (D&C 9:8) BEFORE you ask whether it is right. That means carefully thinking about it, deciding what answer you think is best, and moving forward in faith. Then you can ask Heavenly Father whether that decision is right or wrong.

Sometimes you have to search and act in faith before the answers become clear. Color the sections with dots in them to uncover the hidden picture.

WHEN YOU FEEL THE HOLY GHOST, when you are prompted to do something, or when you get a spiritual insight, write it down! It will help you remember to follow the promptings, and you'll also have a record of all the times the Holy Ghost has touched your life. After you've written down the prompting, ask Heavenly Father if He has anything else He wants you to know, and if He does, write that down too.

Activity: Get a notebook to carry around with you, to write down any spiritual experiences.

Fill in the following list now or pay attention and record next time you feel the Holy Ghost prompting you.

Expert Tip: "Inspiration carefully recorded shows God that His communications are sacred to us. Recording will also enhance our ability to recall revelation." Richard G. Scott, "How to Obtain Revelation and Inspiration for Your Personal Life," *Ensign*, May 2012.

I felt I should do a nice thing for ________________________________.

The nice thing was ________________________________.

I was scared because ____________________, but after I prayed I felt ____________.

Write about a time you did something wrong and the Holy Ghost prompted you to repent and try to fix it: ________________________________.

I felt warm and happy when ________________________________.

Next time you go to the temple grounds, record your feelings.

Today, the Holy Ghost helped me by ________________________________.

How did you feel after bearing your testimony? ________________________.

Today, I prepared to have the Holy Ghost with me by ____________________.

The ways I felt Him were ________________________________.

When I listened to conference I felt inspired to ________________________.

I feel like something I should stop doing is ________________________.

I feel like a good thing I should do is ________________________________.

COLOR-BY-NUMBERS: REVELATION IS LIKE A SUNRISE. Elder Bednar likened revelation to different types of light. Sometimes revelation is like turning on a light switch: the inspiration we receive is instant and clear and comes all at once. However, most of the time, revelation is more like the gradual sunrise: "Most frequently, revelation comes in small increments over time and is granted according to our desire, worthiness, and preparation. Such communications from Heavenly Father gradually and gently 'distil upon [our souls] as the dews from heaven' (D&C 121:45)." (See David A. Bednar, "The Spirit of Revelation," *Ensign*, May 2011.)

1 = Black 2 = Yellow 3 = Orange 4 = Red 5 = Pink
6 = Purple 7 = Light Blue 8 = Blue 9 = Dark Blue 10 = White

Sometimes you have to move forward with faith, knowing only generally, or only one step of what Heavenly Father wants you to do. For this activity, follow the instructions to draw a picture, one step at a time, without knowing what you are drawing. Like your picture, how we act might not be perfect, and we might sometimes misstep or misunderstand. But we move forward trying our best, and God makes up the difference.

INSTRUCTIONS

Using a dark, felt-tip pen, follow the instructions to create a secret picture. For the coordinates, draw lines connecting them in the order listed.

1. c2, c7, d7, d2, c2

2. Above the shape made in 1, draw a tall spike (like a tall triangle).

3. d3, f1, h3, h7, d7

4. e7, e5, g5, g7

5. f5, f7

6. Within these two shapes made in 3, 4, and 5, draw two little door handles.

7. Draw a tree in the two left-hand columns.

8. In an empty square near b2, draw a cloud.

9. In an empty square near h2, draw a cloud.

10. e3, e4, g4, g3, e3

11. Within the shape made in 10, write "The Church of Jesus Christ of Latter-day Saints."

a b c d e f g h i

1 2 3 4 5 6 7 8

See back of book for completed picture.

PROMPTINGS OR ME?

It can seem hard to know whether your thoughts and feelings are from the Holy Ghost or just your own thoughts or feelings. It can take practice to tell them apart. But the easiest way to tell if it is the Spirit communicating with you is to determine whether your inspiration is to do good! If it is, it is from the Spirit.

Can you spot all 16 differences between these two images? In one picture, the children are listening to promptings, in the other picture, some of the children are ignoring the promptings.

You'll often find that you don't get all the answers to your prayers while you are praying. Answers can come any time, but especially while you are engaging in good activities, such as serving others, attending Primary, and choosing the right. It's important to listen to the Holy Ghost while you are praying, but don't get frustrated if you don't feel an answer straight away. Go out, make the best choices you can for yourself, and trust that God will guide you as needed.

Below is the story of Nephi getting the brass plates. Nephi didn't get answers to his prayers right away. He had to go do his best and the Holy Ghost guided him along the way. Number the images in their correct order from 1 to 9.

1. God asked Nephi and his brothers to get the brass plates from wicked Laban.
2. Nephi said he would "go and do the things which the Lord had commanded," even though he didn't know how yet.
3. They asked Laban nicely for the plates, but Laban kicked them out.
4. They got all their treasures, but Laban stole them all and chased after the brothers.
5. Laman and Lemuel wanted to give up. Nephi still had faith.
6. Nephi didn't know what to do, but he did his best until the Holy Ghost guided him.
7. Nephi found Laban drunk and sleeping on the ground. The Spirit told him to kill the wicked Laban.
8. Nephi obeyed. He took Laban's clothes and pretended to be Laban to get the brass plates.
9. Nephi's family was happy to have the scriptures!

Answer Key: A-6, B-8, C-2, D-9, E-4, F-7, G-1, H-5, I-3

GIFTS OF THE SPIRIT

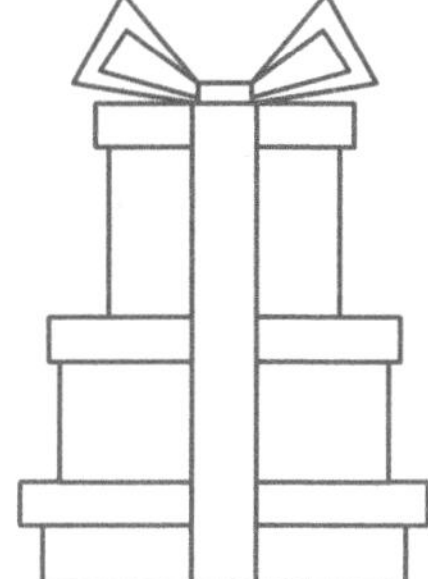

The Holy Ghost's COMPANIONSHIP is a wonderful gift in itself, but He also can bless us with many other spiritual gifts. Heavenly Father expects us to learn which gifts we have been given, and ask the Holy Ghost to help us develop new gifts. These gifts help us become more like Christ, but they are also to help and bless those around us. EVERYONE has been given special spiritual gifts. The Holy Ghost can help you know yours.

Here are explanations of just a few GIFTS OF THE SPIRIT. Color gifts you already think you have. Circle ones you feel you would like to seek.

HERE ARE JUST A FEW:

- **TONGUES:** Learning and understanding languages quickly or speaking the words Heavenly Father wants you to say.
- **HEALING:** Having the faith to be healed after receiving a blessing.
- **KNOWLEDGE:** Learning truth quickly.
- **FAITH:** Believing in important gospel principles.
- **TEACHING:** Effectively teaching other people.
- **HEARING THE SPIRIT:** Recognizing and following the Spirit.
- **BEARING STRONG TESTIMONY:** Sharing your testimony with others.
- **CHARITY:** Feeling Christlike love for others.
- **REVELATION**: Receiving inspiration and guidance from Heavenly Father.
- **DISCERNMENT:** Knowing good influences from bad influences.
- **PEACEMAKER**: Avoiding contention and helping others feel peaceful.

Jesus told a parable about a man who gave his servants some coins called talents. Two of the servants worked hard to use those talents to get more talents. One of the servants was too scared to do anything, so he hid his talent. The man who gave the coins was only happy with the two men who increased their talents, and he gave them more. He took away the talent of the man who had wasted his. Heavenly Father wants us to use the talents he has given us to gain more talents!

FIGURING OUT WHAT'S WRONG

Expert Tip: "You cannot force spiritual things. Such words as compel, coerce, constrain, pressure, and demand do not describe our privileges with the Spirit. You can no more force the Spirit to respond than you can force a bean to sprout or an egg to hatch before its time. You can create a climate to foster growth, nourish, and protect; but you cannot force or compel: you must await the growth." Boyd K. Packer, "The Candle of the Lord," *Ensign*, Jan. 1983.

Sometimes it can seem like the Holy Ghost isn't communicating with us. This page can help you figure out why.

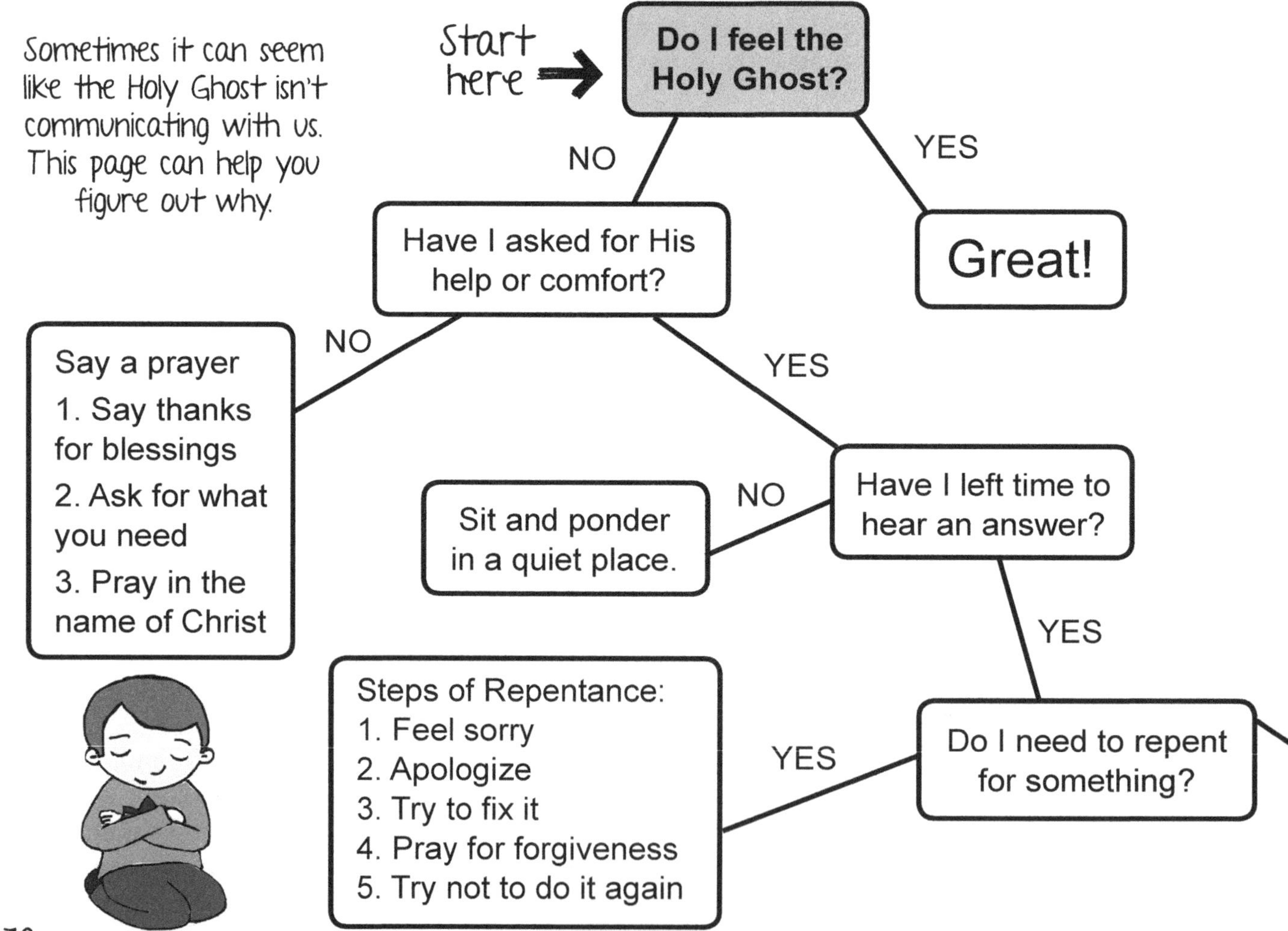

Go forward in faith. Have patience. Consider that Heavenly Father trusts you to make your own decision. Do what you think is best and listen to impressions as you act in faith.

NO

Am I expecting the wrong thing? Am I hoping for a voice or a strong impression, when the Holy Ghost is actually giving me a feeling or thought in His still, small voice?

YES

Try to pay attention to the different ways the Holy Ghost can guide you. He most often speaks in thoughts and feelings.

YES

Have I done things to invite the Spirit to be with me?

NO

Try reading the scriptures, listening to uplifting music, serving others, and pondering and thinking about the gospel.

YES

NO

Are you in a place the Holy Ghost would want to be?

NO

Find somewhere peaceful, quiet, and clean where you can be alone.

CONCLUSION

Congratulations! You've almost completed this book! We hope it has been a wonderful experience. Always remember that Heavenly Father loves you, and He always wants to help and guide you. He will never leave you alone. The Holy Ghost is one of His greatest gifts for you. The Holy Ghost will guide you, comfort you, teach you, warn you, and help you repent and become like Christ. As you have faith, you will learn to hear and respond to the Holy Ghost, until He can constantly be with you. Never give up, even when it seems hard. Learning to recognize the Holy Ghost is a lifelong process, but it is a process that will change your entire life!

JOSEPH LEARNS A LESSON

WHEN JOSEPH ARRIVED AT SCHOOL....

EVERYONE IS LEAVING!
JOSEPH FINDS HIMSELF COMPLETELY ON HIS OWN....
I DON'T KNOW WHAT TO DO....
JOSEPH? YOU'RE IN HERE!
NOT A GREAT START, JOSEPH. DON'T BE LATE TOMORROW.
HE'S CRYING!!
HA! HA! HA!
OH! I'VE MADE MYSELF LOOK STUPID. NOW, NO ONE WILL BE MY FRIEND.
PSST..
OH! THANKS!
I want my Mommy
Boo hoo
Boo hoo
STUPID cry baby
I AM STUPID.
THINGS DIDN'T GET ANY BETTER AT LUNCH TIME...
HEY! THERE'S THE NEW KID!
OH DEAR! OOOOPS!
HA! HA
AGGHHH!
SMAASH!

AT THE END OF SCHOOL, JOSEPH WALKED SADLY HOME...

LATER THAT NIGHT AT FAMILY HOME EVENING....
SO, TELL ME.. WHAT SPECIAL GIFT HAVE WE BEEN GIVEN THAT HELPS US?
OOH! I KNOW! ROSIE! I LOVE HER!
WELL...YES, SHE WAS A SPECIAL GIFT, BUT THE ONE I'M TALKING ABOUT IS GIVEN TO YOU WHEN YOU ARE BAPTIZED....?
"JOSEPH?"
IT'S THE GIFT OF THE HOLY GHOST. IT HELPS US COPE WITH LIFE WHEN IT GET'S REALLY HARD. WE CAN FEEL PEACE, CALM, AND COURAGE. IT HELPS US TO COPE. WOULD YOU LIKE THAT?
OOH! YES!
GOOD! BUT WE MUST DO OUR PART, WHAT DO YOU THINK THAT MAY BE..?
I KNOW! NOT HIT PEOPLE!
WE CERTAINLY SHOULDN'T HIT PEOPLE, CAITLIN, WE ALSO NEED TO BE OBEDIENT! TO PRAY, TO TRY OUR BEST, AND TO LISTEN TO YOUR FEELINGS.
"WHO WOULD LIKE TO READ ALMA 37:40?"
AND IT DID WORK FOR THEM ACCORDING TO THEIR FAITH...THEREFORE THEY HAD THIS MIRACLE, AND... MANY OTHER MIRACLES... BY THE POWER OF GOD, DAY BY DAY.
EXACTLY! JUST LIKE THE LIAHONA, THE HOLY GHOST WORKS EXACTLY THE SAME WAY! WE CAN RECEIVE MIRACLES EVERY DAY OF OUR LIVES - IF WE ARE OBEDIENT AND HAVE FAITH - IF WE BELIEVE!
"I HAVE A LITTLE LIAHONA FOR EACH OF YOU. WHEN YOU LOOK AT THESE THEN YOU CAN REMEMBER THAT YOU ARE NEVER ALONE. YOU HAVE BEEN GIVEN A GIFT THAT CAN BE YOUR BEST FRIEND..."
OOH!

WILL YOU KEEP THESE CLOSE TO YOU, SO YOU WILL ALWAYS REMEMBER THAT YOU ARE NEVER, EVER ALONE? NO MATTER HOW HARD LIFE MAY SEEM, YOU ARE GOING TO BE ALRIGHT. YOU CAN BE BRAVE AND FACE THOSE CHALLENGES!
YES, YES I WILL, DAD!
"JOSEPH?"
OK, DAD.
IT WONT WORK FOR ME. MY PROBLEMS ARE TOO HARD.
JOSEPH!
WELL, HERE WE GO AGAIN.
"WE CAN RECEIVE MIRACLES EVERY DAY IF WE BELIEVE."
I GUESS IT'S WORTH A TRY...
DEAR HEAVENLY FATHER. PLEASE HELP ME TO BE BRAVE... AND TO MAKE A NEW FRIEND.
DID YOU SAY YOUR PRAYERS, JOSEPH?
YES! LOVE YOU, MUM!
I CAN DO THIS!
HEY, STUPID! ARE YOU GOING TO CRY TODAY?
MAYBE I AM STUPID....
NO! I AM NOT! I'M NOT STUPID.
I WILL NOT LISTEN TO HIS MEAN WORDS.
OUT OF MY WAY, SHORTIE.
POOR GUY!....BUT IF I HELP HIM, I'LL GET THEM TEASING ME AGAIN, I DON'T NEED THAT RIGHT NOW...
WHAT SHALL I DO?

NO! I NEED TO HELP HIM, IT'S THE RIGHT THING TO DO!
HERE! LET ME HELP YOU UP...
OH... THANKS.
I'M JOSEPH.
I KNOW, I'M IN YOUR CLASS. I'M MATTHEW.
DO YOU WANT TO SIT WITH ME AT LUNCH?
HEY! THE TWO CRY BABIES HAVING LUNCH! HOW SWEET! HA! HA! HA!
"OH NO!"
DON'T WORRY ABOUT THEM. LET'S IGNORE THEIR MEAN WORDS.
OH. OK!
HI MATTHEW, CAN WE SIT WITH YOU?
HI, JOSEPH, I'M EVE.
I'M WILLIAM.
WE'RE SO SORRY YOU HAD SUCH A HORRIBLE DAY YESTERDAY.
WOW! IT REALLY WORKED! EVERYTHING IS GOING TO BE OK!!
HI, JOSEPH. HOW WAS YOUR DAY?
GREAT, MUM! I MADE THREE NEW FRIENDS!
DAD WAS RIGHT!
THE HOLY GHOST HELPED ME BE BRAVE.
HE TRULY IS MY GREATEST GIFT!
THE END

ANSWER KEY

The Holy Ghost Can Guide You to Find Missing Things hidden items, page 24

Promptings or Me? find 16 differences, pages 66-67

Names of the Holy Ghost fill in the blanks, page 19

Holy Spirit
Spirit of God
Spirit of the Lord
Comforter
Still, small voice
Holy Spirit of Promise

Test Your Gospel Knowledge questions, page 47

1. John the Baptist 2. 14
3. Abinadi 4. 13 5. Moses
6. 1 Nephi 7. Noah
8. Joseph Smith

Names of the Holy Ghost word search, page 19

W	X	S	E	E	T	A	N	O	E	P	E	L	D	T
E	I	G	A	L	E	W	S	Z	N	N	H	Q	T	E
T	D	U	S	N	A	K	X	E	M	D	L	M	J	P
M	C	I	P	G	C	S	H	D	D	O	M	P	Z	D
F	O	D	R	T	H	T	Y	N	N	A	C	D	S	E
T	M	E	O	E	G	U	I	I	H	Z	N	W	D	F
R	F	M	T	N	C	M	E	F	S	O	A	H	P	O
N	O	Y	E	M	E	T	I	T	Y	F	E	S	E	M
T	R	R	C	R	W	E	B	I	E	E	F	O	L	O
E	T	E	T	D	A	V	E	M	O	S	B	S	N	C
S	E	H	V	A	R	T	R	J	F	X	F	U	P	Q
T	H	T	E	E	N	X	R	P	I	C	B	E	A	K
I	H	I	F	E	A	E	O	Y	L	A	T	L	E	T
F	R	M	M	N	P	L	N	T	A	S	J	A	S	A
Y	S	H	E	N	A	S	Q	F	E	M	I	R	T	E

Completed Picture, page 65

a b c d e f g h i

1 2 3 4 5 6 7 8

The Church of Jesus Christ of Latter-day Saints

Guess the Picture, page 59